Mel Bay's
STUDENT'S GUIDE TO MUSIC THEORY

A Book of Music Fundamentals for Students

by L. Dean Bye

Contents

Musical Notation And Pitch

THE STAFF: Music is written on a STAFF consisting of FIVE LINES and FOUR SPACES.

The lines and spaces are numbered upward as shown:

5TH LINE	
4TH LINE	4TH SPACE
3RD LINE	3RD SPACE
2ND LINE	2ND SPACE
1ST LINE	1ST SPACE

THE LINES AND SPACES ARE NAMED AFTER LETTERS OF THE ALPHABET.

THE TREBLE CLEF:

 This sign is the treble or G Clef.

The second line of the treble clef is known as the G line. Many people call the treble clef the G clef because it circles around the G line.

The LINES in the Treble Clef are named as follows:

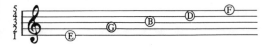

The letters may easily be remembered by the sentence - **E**very **G**ood **B**oy **D**oes **F**ine

The letter - names of the SPACES in the Treble Clef are:

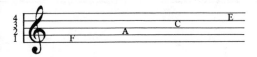

They spell the word F - A - C - E

The Musical Alphabet has <u>seven</u> letters - A B C D E F G

On a separate piece of manuscript paper, practice writing "G" or Treble clef signs.

THE BASS CLEF:

This sign is the bass or F clef.

As we can see, the fourth line of the bass clef is known as the "F" line. Many people call the bass clef the F clef because the two dots are placed on either side of the line. All other letter names are figured from this line.

The Lines on the Bass Clef are named as follows:

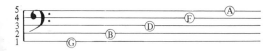

These letters may easily be remembered by the sentence - <u>G</u>ood <u>B</u>oys <u>D</u>o <u>F</u>ine <u>A</u>lways

The letter - names of the spaces in the Bass Clef are:

These letters may be remembered by the sentence - <u>A</u>ll <u>C</u>ars <u>E</u>at <u>G</u>as

<u>Leger</u> <u>lines</u> are short lines placed above and below the staff. Some examples are:

On a separate sheet of Manuscript Paper, practice writing "F" or Bass Clef Signs.

When both the treble and bass clefs are combined with an added leger line (middle C) it is known as the grand staff.

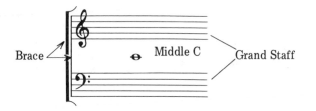

The perpendicular line and the bracket that joins two or more different staves is called a <u>brace.</u>

Staff Notation And Keyboard Position:

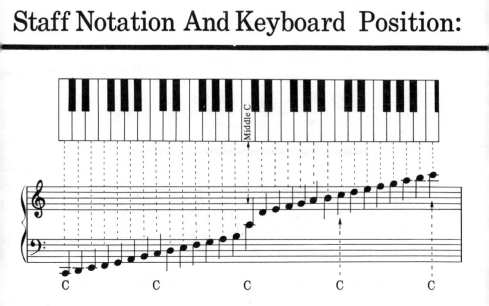

Staff Notation And Guitar Position

The six open strings of the guitar will be of the same pitch as the six notes shown in the illustration of the piano keyboard. Note that five of the strings are below the middle C of the piano keyboard.

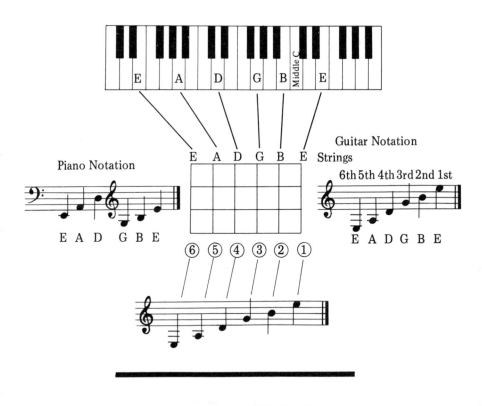

DRILL in the letter names of notes and REVIEW of the staff location must be continued until they are learned!

(For more detailed work on music notation and pitch, See <u>Theory and Harmony for Everyone</u> published by Mel Bay Publications, Inc.)

Musical Notation And Pitch

(Review)

1. The musical staff consists of _____ lines and _____ spaces.

2. Draw a treble clef and label the lines and spaces on the following staff.

3. Draw a bass clef and label the lines and spaces on the following staff.

4. The _____ staff consists of the _____ and _____ clefs along with middle C.

5. The _____ _____ determines the letter names of the lines and spaces.

6. Write the letter names under the following notes.

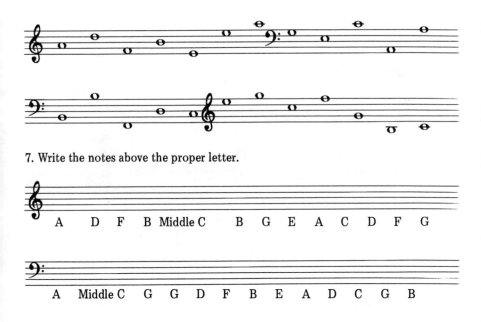

7. Write the notes above the proper letter.

A   D   F   B Middle C   B   G   E   A   C   D   F   G

A   Middle C   G   G   D   F   B   E   A   D   C   G   B

Duration Of Notes And Rests--Meter

TONE:

A TONE has four characteristics ... PITCH, DURATION, DYNAMICS and TIMBRE.

PITCH: The highness or lowness of a tone.

DURATION: The length of a tone.

DYNAMICS: The force or power of a tone. (Loudness or softness.)

TIMBRE: Quality of the tone.

A NOTE represents the PITCH AND DURATION of a tone.

NOTES:

This is a note:

A note has three parts. They are

The HEAD ⟶

The STEM ⟶

The FLAG ⟶

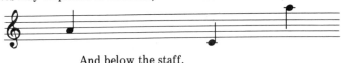

Notes may be placed in the staff;   Above the staff;

And below the staff.

A note will bear the name of the line or space it occupies on the staff. The location of a note in, above, or below the staff will indicate the Pitch.

PITCH: The height or depth of a tone.

TONE: A musical sound.

REMEMBER: A Note represents the Pitch and Duration of a tone and it will bear the name of the line or space it occupies on the staff.

8

TYPES OF NOTES:

THE TYPE OF NOTE WILL INDICATE THE LENGTH OF ITS SOUND.

𝐨 This is a whole note.
The head is hollow.
It does not have a stem.

𝐨 = 4 Beats
A whole note will receive
4 beats or counts.

𝅗𝅥 This is a half note.
The head is hollow.
It has a stem.

𝅗𝅥 = 2 Beats
A half note will receive
2 beats or counts.

♩ This is a quarter note.
The head is solid.
It has a stem.

♩ = 1 Beat
A quarter note will receive
1 beat or count.

♪ This is an eighth note.
The head is solid.
It has a stem and a flag.

♪ = ½ Beat
An eighth note will receive
one - half beat or count.
(2 for 1 beat)

RESTS:

A REST is a sign used to designate a period of silence.

This period of silence will be of the same duration of time as the note to which it corresponds.

𝄾 This is an eighth rest. 　　　　𝄽 This is a quarter rest.

▬ This is a half rest. Note that it sits on the line.

▬ This is a whole rest. Note that it hangs down from the line.

NOTES:	𝐨	𝅗𝅥	♩	♪
	Whole 4 Counts	Half 2 Counts	Quarter 1 Count	Eighth 2 for Count
RESTS:	▬	▬	𝄽	𝄾

When the head of a note is placed above the third line, the stem is usually drawn downward on the left side of the note. When the head of the note is located below the third line the stem usually goes upward on the right side. Notes <u>on</u> the third line may have stems going either way.

<u>A</u> <u>Dot</u> <u>After</u> <u>A</u> <u>Note</u> (or a rest) increases its value by <u>one-half</u>. See the following examples.

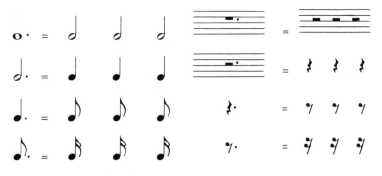

A Quick Review:

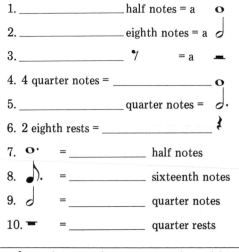

1. _____ half notes = a 𝅝

2. _____ eighth notes = a 𝅗𝅥

3. _____ 𝄿 = a ▬

4. 4 quarter notes = _____ 𝅝

5. _____ quarter notes = 𝅗𝅥.

6. 2 eighth rests = _____ 𝄾

7. 𝅝. = _____ half notes

8. 𝅘𝅥𝅯. = _____ sixteenth notes

9. 𝅗𝅥 = _____ quarter notes

10. ▬ = _____ quarter rests

On a separate sheet of manuscript paper, practice writing different note and rest values.

The STAFF is divided into measures by vertical lines called BARS.

BAR   BAR

MEASURE   MEASURE   MEASURE

Heavy double bars mark the end of a section or strain of music.*

* A division <u>within</u> a piece or movement is shown by a light double bar.

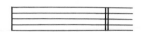

Note: A <u>measure</u> is the space between two bar lines.

The Time Signature

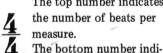

The above examples are common types of time signatures.

 The top number indicates the number of beats per measure.
The bottom number indicates the type of note receiving one beat.

 Example:

 Beats per measure
A quarter-note receives one beat

 Signifies so called "common time" and simply another way of designating $\frac{4}{4}$ time.

The symbol for cut time is . It means to give each note ½ of its written value. For our purposes all we need remember is that when the time signature ¢ appears, we will count $\frac{2}{2}$ instead of $\frac{4}{4}$ or C .

On a separate sheet of manuscript paper, practice writing a number of meter (Time Signature) examples.

TEMPO

Tempo is the rate of movement or speed of a piece of music. Tempo is indicated by a word or phrase which is very often in Italian.

Some of the most important of these terms are given in the chart below. They are arranged in order from slowest to fastest.*

BASIC TEMPO MARKINGS

Largo - Very slow and stately.

Largamente - Broadly. Quite slow.

Larghetto - Faster than Largo, but slow.

Grave - Seriously, solemn.

Lento - Slowly (often used temporarily)

Adagio - Slowly, very expressive

Andante - Tranquilly, but moving right along.

Andantino - Generally interpreted as slightly faster than Andante.

Moderato - Moderately. It is usually considered the medium point between the slowest and fastest markings.

Allegretto - Animated, but less than Allegro

Allegro - Lively, animated in movement.

Vivace - More rapidly than Allegro.

Presto - Very fast.

Prestissimo - The fastest tempo used.

*Tempo is measured with a metronome, a mechanical (or electric) device for determining the number of beats to be played at the tempo indicated by the composer. Set the metronome using the various tempo markings from the above list and listen so that a feeling for these may be established. Specific metronome markings may appear also as the following examples show.

m.m. ♩ = 70 Seventy metronome beats per minute; a quarter note receives one beat.

m.m. ♩ = 40 Forty metronome beats per minute; a half note receives one beat.

On a preceding page we learned that we could change $\frac{4}{4}$ (common) time to $\frac{2}{2}$ (cut) time. We can perform a similar change from "slow time" to "fast time" for $\frac{3}{8}$ $\frac{6}{8}$ $\frac{9}{8}$ $\frac{12}{8}$ time by dividing both the top number of beats per measure and the value of the eighth note by 3, giving the eighth note (♪) $\frac{1}{3}$ beat.

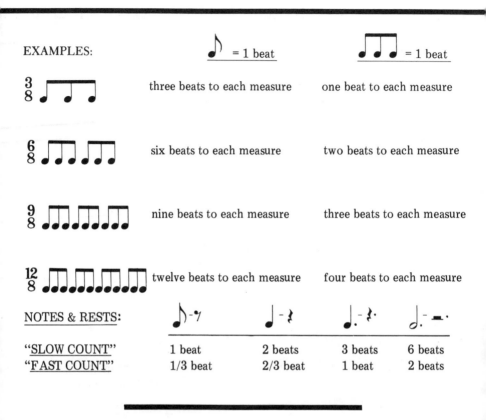

EXAMPLES:	♪ = 1 beat	♪♪♪ = 1 beat
3/8 ♪♪♪	three beats to each measure	one beat to each measure
6/8 ♪♪♪ ♪♪♪	six beats to each measure	two beats to each measure
9/8 ♪♪♪♪♪♪♪♪♪	nine beats to each measure	three beats to each measure
12/8 ♪♪♪♪♪♪♪♪♪♪♪♪	twelve beats to each measure	four beats to each measure

NOTES & RESTS:

	♪ - 𝄾	♩ - 𝄿	♩. - 𝄾.	𝅗𝅥. - ▬.
"SLOW COUNT"	1 beat	2 beats	3 beats	6 beats
"FAST COUNT"	1/3 beat	2/3 beat	1 beat	2 beats

SYNCOPATION: Special rhythmic effects may be acquired in music by placing special accents (>) or emphasis on different beats or parts of a beat. If a natural accent or strong beat is moved from its normal place to a weak beat, we have syncopation. This could be done a number of ways. Study the following examples for some of them. (The accent marks are to show where syncopation occurs.)

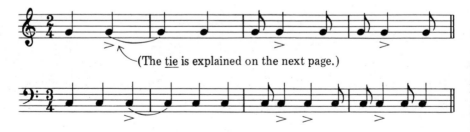

(The tie is explained on the next page.)

THE TIE:

The **TIE** is a curved line between two notes of the same pitch.
The first note is played and held for the time duration of both.
The second note is not played but held.

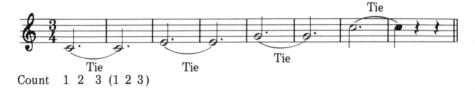

Count   1   2   3   (1   2   3)

Complex Time Signatures

Some of the more complex time signatures which are presently in use are:

$$\frac{3}{2} \qquad \frac{5}{4} \qquad \frac{7}{4} \qquad \frac{9}{4} \qquad \frac{5}{8} \qquad \frac{7}{8}$$

Remember: In every case the top number always tells the number of beats in a measure, and the bottom number always tells the kind of note that gets one beat.

(For additional work on Rhythm and Tempo See <u>Theory and Harmony</u> for <u>Everyone</u> published by Mel Bay Publications, Inc.)

Duration Of Notes And Rests--Meter
(Review)

1. Draw the missing bar lines in the following exercise.

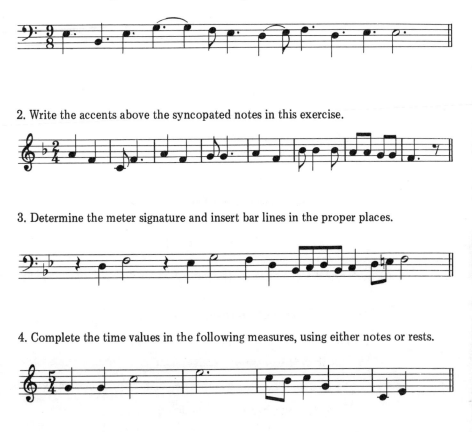

2. Write the accents above the syncopated notes in this exercise.

3. Determine the meter signature and insert bar lines in the proper places.

4. Complete the time values in the following measures, using either notes or rests.

Remember: <u>Syncopation</u> means to accent tones, or beats, which are normally unaccented.

Key Signatures- Major/Minor Scales

A <u>half</u> <u>step</u> is the distance from one pitch (tone) to the next nearest pitch (tone) either up or down. This interval is often referred to as a <u>semitone</u>.

Examples: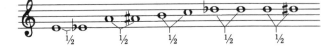

A <u>whole</u> <u>step</u> is two adjacent half steps. This interval is often referred to as a <u>whole</u> <u>tone</u>.

Examples:

ACCIDENTALS:

There are signs called accidentals which, when placed before a note, alter the pitch of the note.

♯ Sharp: raises pitch a half-step

♭ Flat: lowers pitch a half-step

× Double-Sharp: raises pitch two half-steps, or one whole-step

♭♭ Double-Flat: lowers pitch two half-steps or one whole-step

♮ Natural: cancels a sharp or a flat

Accidentals affect only the tones within that octave register and within that measure.

On a separate sheet of manuscript paper, practice writing examples of the above shown accidentals.

Key Signatures

Sharps and flats immediately following the clef sign are called the <u>key</u> signature. These accidentals affect every note on the line or space which they represent throughout the entire composition unless they are cancelled by a natural sign (♮) or a change to another key.

In the following example, every note called F is now raised one half-step to F♯ because a sharp is placed on the F line in the key signature.

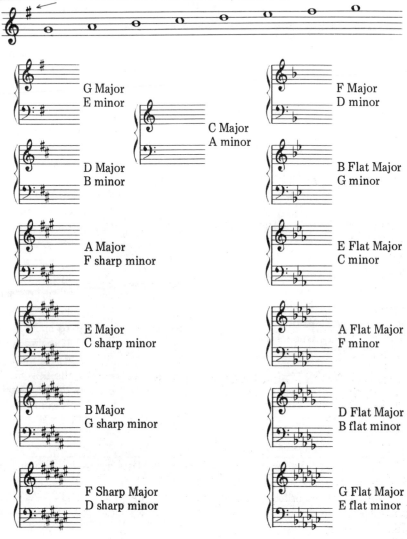

G Major
E minor

F Major
D minor

C Major
A minor

D Major
B minor

B Flat Major
G minor

A Major
F sharp minor

E Flat Major
C minor

E Major
C sharp minor

A Flat Major
F minor

B Major
G sharp minor

D Flat Major
B flat minor

F Sharp Major
D sharp minor

G Flat Major
E flat minor

17

A Diatonic Scale is a series of eight successive notes (the eighth duplicating the first) that are arranged in a systematic relationship of whole and half steps.

The diatonic scale is made up of two types - - Major and Minor.

Building A Major Scale

A major scale is a series of eight notes arranged in this pattern of whole steps and half steps.

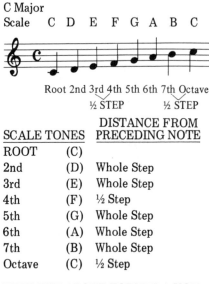

C Major
Scale   C   D   E   F   G   A   B   C

Root 2nd 3rd 4th 5th 6th 7th Octave
½ STEP   ½ STEP

SCALE TONES		DISTANCE FROM PRECEDING NOTE
ROOT	(C)	
2nd	(D)	Whole Step
3rd	(E)	Whole Step
4th	(F)	½ Step
5th	(G)	Whole Step
6th	(A)	Whole Step
7th	(B)	Whole Step
Octave	(C)	½ Step

WITH THE ABOVE FORMULA YOU CAN CONSTRUCT ANY MAJOR SCALE!

To construct a major scale we first start with the name of the scale (Frequently called the Root or Tonic).

With the C scale this would be the note "C." The rest of the scale would fall in line as follows:

C to D = Whole Step | G to A = Whole Step
D to E = Whole Step | A to B = Whole Step
E to F = ½ Step | B to C = ½ Step
F to G = Whole Step |

G MAJOR SCALE

To construct the G major scale, start with the note G, construct it as follows:

G   A   B   C   D   E   F♯   G

Root 2nd 3rd 4th 5th 6th 7th Octave
½ STEP   ½ STEP

Notice that in order to make our formula work with the G scale we must sharp(♯) the F. There must be a whole step between the 6th and 7th tones of the scale. In order to establish a whole step between E and F we must sharp the F.

Remember: The combination of sharps and flats necessary to form a major scale is called a key signature.

Notice that the order of flats is opposite to the order to sharps.

F♯   C♯   G♯   D♯   A♯   E♯   B♯
B♭   E♭   A♭   D♭   G♭   C♭   F♭

Table Of Major Keys And Signatures

C MAJOR has no sharps or flats

G MAJOR has one sharp,	F♯					
D MAJOR has two sharps,	F♯	C♯				
A MAJOR has three sharps,	F♯	C♯	G♯			
E MAJOR has four sharps,	F♯	C♯	G♯	D♯		
B MAJOR has five sharps,	F♯	C♯	G♯	D♯	A♯	
F♯ MAJOR has six sharps,	F♯	C♯	G♯	D♯	A♯	E♯
C♯ MAJOR has seven sharps,	F♯	C♯	G♯	D♯	A♯	E♯	B♯

F MAJOR has one flat,	B♭					
B♭ MAJOR has two flats,	B♭	E♭				
E♭ MAJOR has three flats,	B♭	E♭	A♭			
A♭ MAJOR has four flats,	B♭	E♭	A♭	D♭		
D♭ MAJOR has five flats,	B♭	E♭	A♭	D♭	G♭	
G♭ MAJOR has six flats,	B♭	E♭	A♭	D♭	G♭	C♭
C♭ MAJOR has seven flats,	B♭	E♭	A♭	D♭	G♭	C♭	F♭

The following diagram of the cycle of keys shows the relationship of all the major scales.

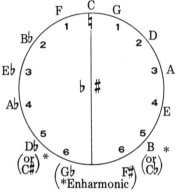

The most important degrees in each key are 1 - 3 - 5 which form the Tonic or I chord of the key.

Write the 1 - 3 - 5 or <u>Tonic</u> of the following keys:
C, G, F, A, E♭, and B.

STARTING WITH C MOVING TO THE RIGHT GIVES US THE KEYS CONTAINING SHARPS AND MOVING TO THE LEFT GIVES US THE KEYS CONTAINING FLATS.

*Enharmonic: Written differently as to notation but sounding the same.

Minor Scales

Each Major key will have a Relative Minor key.
The Relative Minor Scale is built upon the sixth tone of the Major Scale.
The Key Signature of both will be the same.
The Minor Scale will have the same number of tones (7) as the Major.
The difference between the scales is the arrangement of the whole-steps and half-steps.
There are three forms of the minor scale: 1. PURE or NATURAL, 2. HARMONIC, 3. MELODIC.

THE MAJOR AND RELATIVE MINOR KEYS:

D is the 6th Tone of the F Scale; G is the 6th Tone of the B Scale, etc.

		C	Am		
F	Dm		F♯	D♯m	
B♭	Gm		B	G♯m	
E♭	Cm		E	C♯m	
A♭	Fm		A	F♯m	
D♭	B♭m		D	Bm	
G♭	E♭m		G	Em	

The NATURAL or PURE MINOR SCALE begins on the 6th degree of its relative major scale and ascends or descends for one octave using the key signature of the major scale. We usually use small letters to indicate minor keys. The half steps occur between 2-3 and 5-6.

c minor (natural)

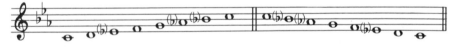

The HARMONIC MINOR SCALE begins on the 6th degree of its relative major scale and ascends or descends for one octave using the key signature of the major scale except that the 7th tone is raised 1/2 step. (See arrow in the example below) The half steps occur between 2-3, and 7-8.*

c minor (harmonic)

*The raised seventh scale tone in the harmonic minor creates the distance of a step and one half between 6-7.

The MELODIC MINOR SCALE also begins on the 6th degree of its relative major scale and ascends or descends for one octave using the key signature of the major scale except that in ascending the 6th and 7th tones are raised 1/2 step and in descending the 6th and 7th tones return to the natural or pure minor scale form.*

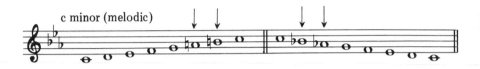

*In the melodic minor ascending, the half steps occur between the 2-3 and 7-8 notes

> On a separate sheet of manuscript paper, construct the minor scale for each key and label the Root, Third, and Fifth tones of each scale. Show both the ascending and descending forms of the melodic minor. Finally, write the sharps or flats found in each key signature.

A CHROMATIC SCALE is a scale which consists entirely of half steps. It may be written by the use of accidentals (♯-♭-♮) in connection with the regular key signature. Sharp and natural signs are used for the ascending scale and flat and natural signs for the descending scale.

The filled-in notes designate the ascending and descending chromatic tones in C major in the following example:

> On a separate sheet of manuscript paper, write an ascending chromatic scale in the key of E♭ a and a descending chromatic scale in the key of A. Remember -- frequent drill in any musical skill is necessary.

*Notice that the chromatic scale has a number of enharmonic tones (see page 19). The term enharmonic pertains to tones which are "Spelled" differently but sound the same. For example: a♭-g♯; c♭-b; e♭-d♯; and f♭-e.

Key Signatures– Major/Minor Scales
(Review)

1. Put in the clef sign, write the proper key signature and place the starting note of the scale in the following exercises.

Treble Clef

A   G♭   B   E♭

Bass Clef

D   B♭   A   G♭

2. Using half notes write the MAJOR SCALES ascending and descending for the following key signatures.

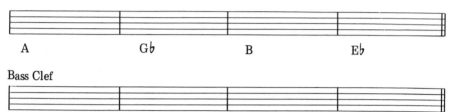

3. Determine the relative minor keys of the following Major Keys. (use small letters and proper accidentals.)

Major Scale	Relative minor Scale		Major Scale	Relative minor Scale
C	a		G	___
F	___		D	___
B♭	___		A	___
E♭	___		E	___
A♭	___		B	___
D♭	___		F♯	___

4. Name the following Major Scales; then name and write the relative minor scale of each, as indicated, both ascending and descending.

Key of _____ major   Key of _____ minor (harmonic)

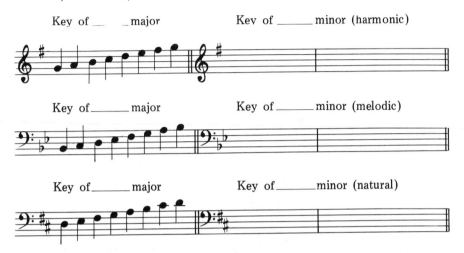

Key of _____ major   Key of _____ minor (melodic)

Key of _____ major   Key of _____ minor (natural)

5. On the staff below, write the enharmonic note in the second measure.

6. How many notes are there in a chromatic scale including the octave?_____

7. What is the interval between the tones of the chromatic scale?_____

(For additional information On Key Signatures and Scales, See <u>Theory and Harmony for Everyone</u> published by Mel Bay Publications, Inc.)

Form And Expression Marks

In order to read, write, or understand music, one must know all of the signs, words and abbreviations which are often referred to as the musical vocabulary. Many of these have been given on other pages, but most are included here.

1. A <u>melody</u> is a succession of single tones.

2. A <u>chord</u> is a combination of tones sounded together.

3. A <u>triad</u> is a three note chord.

           Tones in a melody.   The same tones as a chord.

4. A <u>phrase</u> is a short musical thought - - a musical sentence. The phrase usually finishes on a note of longer duration, or at the end of a rhythmic pattern. A double bar does not necessarily mean the beginning or end of a phrase.

Example:

5. A <u>period</u> is a "complete musical thought" usually made up of two phrases.

Example:

6. A <u>slur</u> is a curved line drawn above or below groups of two or more notes. Usually this means that the notes are to be played or sung <u>legato</u> (Smoothly).

Example:

7. A <u>tie</u> is a curved line connecting two notes of the same letter name and pitch.

Example:

8. When sections or portions of a piece of music are to be repeated, various signs are used.

(A) <u>D.C. (Da Capo)</u> means to repeat from the beginning to the word <u>Fine</u> (the end).

Example: (A B A)

(B) <u>D.S. (Dal Segno)</u> means to repeat <u>from</u> <u>the</u> <u>Sign</u> (𝄋) to the word <u>Fine</u> (the end).

Example: (A B C B)

(C) Two dots before a double barline mean to return to the beginning or to another double bar followed by two dots.

Example: (A A B B)

(D) <u>First and second endings</u> are often used after repetitions in music.

Example: (A B A C)

9. DYNAMICS are indicated by words such as . . .

Pianissimo . . . . (pp) . . . . Very soft
Piano . . . . (p) . . . . Soft
Mezzo piano . . . .(mp) . . . . Medium soft
Mezzo forte . . . . (mf) . . . . Medium loud
Forte . . . . (f) . . . . loud
Fortissimo . . . . (ff) . . . . Very loud

10. The names of all scale degrees in a diatonic scale are:
First Degree - Tonic
Second Degree - Supertonic
Third Degree - Mediant
Fourth Degree - Subdominant
Fifth Degree - Dominant
Sixth Degree - Submediant
Seventh Degree - Leading Tone
Eighth Degree - Octave

Expression Marks/Abbreviations

ad lib. - giving the performer liberty in matters of tempo and express-ion.

Accel. - Accelerando (increase speed or tempo)

$\overset{>}{\uparrow}$ Accent - to stress or to emphasize

Accom. - Accompaniment

a tempo - resume strict time

← A double bar - line
A bar - line

$\lor$, ' - Breath marks

⊕ - Coda

< or cresc, - crescendo (get louder)

• - Dot
   1) a dot placed after a note or rest increases the value one half. (Exp. ♩.)
   2) a dot placed below or above a note indicates that the note should be played <u>staccato</u>. (Exp. ♩)

> or Dim. - Diminuendo or Decresc. (get softer)

⌒ - a fermata or <u>hold</u>

Fine - the end

♪ (Subdivide) - in this case play four eighth notes.

Leg. - Legato (smoothly and connected)
meno - less
ped. - pedal
piu - more
rall. - rallentando (gradually slower)
repeat - a character indicating that certain measures or passages are to be sung or played twice.
(see previous page)

rit. - ritard or ritardando (gradually slower)

rubato - a flexibility of tempo-a quicken-ing and slowing of the tempo by the performer or conductor.

sforzando (sfz) - a strong accent - imme-diately followed by piano (soft).

♯ ; ♭ ; ♮ - sharp; flat; natural

✕ - Double - Sharp; raises the pitch two half - steps or one whole step.

♭♭ - Double - flat; lowers the pitch two half steps or one whole step.

Sign - a note or character employed in music.

Spiccato - Italian for very detached. (usually used for string instru-ments.)

≡ - a staff

Suspension - the holding of a note in any chord into the chord which follows

♩ or ten. - tenuto - sustain for full value.

Triplet - ♪♪♪ - a group of three notes performed in the time of 2.

Tutti - <u>All</u> - Everyone sings or plays.

Unis. - Unison

Vamp - to improvise an accompaniment

8va. - 8 notes higher

Voce (It.) - the voice

Volume - The power (loudness or softness) of a voice or instrument

Whole step - two half steps or a major second

Form And Expression Marks

(Review)

1. A three note chord is called a _____ .

2. A succession of single tones is called a _____ .

3. A phrase is _____ .

4. A period is _____ .

5. Match the following by putting the correct letter in the blank.

_____ Mezzo forte	A. very loud
_____ Piano	B. very soft
_____ Mezzo piano	C. med. loud
_____ Forte	D. med. soft
_____ Pianissimo	E. soft
_____ Fortissimo	F. loud

6. Match the following terms with the correct definitions.

_____ slur   A. repeat from the beginning to the word Fine

_____ chord   B. 8 notes higher

_____ Dal Segno (D.S.)   C. curved line drawn above or below groups of two or

_____ tie   more notes.

_____ a tempo   D. strong accent immediately followed by piano (p)

_____ rall.   E. gradually slower

_____ Tutti   F. combination of tones sounded together

_____ 8va.   G. get softer

_____ volume   H. All - everyone sings or plays

_____ ad. lib. >   I. curved line connecting two notes of the same letter

_____ accent   name and pitch

_____ crescendo ⟨ J. giving the performer liberty of tempo and expression

_____ sforzando(sf^z)   K. resume strict time

_____ decrescendo ⟩ L. repeat from the sign (𝄋) to the word Fine

_____ Da Capo (D.C.)   M. loudness or softness of a voice or instrument

                              N. to stress or emphasize

Intervals And Two-Part Harmony

An <u>interval</u> in music is the distance between two tones with regard to pitch. The interval is counted from the lower note to the upper, including both notes. Intervals remain the same whether we use the bass clef or the treble clef.

Intervals played or written together are called Harmonic.

Intervals played or written one after another are called Melodic.

INTERVALS IN THE SCALE OF C MAJOR

Prime or Unison	Second	Third	Fourth	Fifth	Sixth	Seventh	Octave
Perfect	Major	Major	Perfect	Perfect	Major	Major	Perfect

> An Interval is Major when the upper note is found in the major scale of the lower note.

> When the distance between two notes of a Major interval is made one half step smaller, it is called a MINOR INTERVAL.

Only SECONDS – THIRDS – SIXTHS – SEVENTHS or Major intervals can be made minor.

Examples:

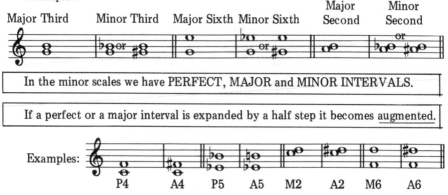

Major Third	Minor Third	Major Sixth	Minor Sixth	Major Second	Minor Second

> In the minor scales we have PERFECT, MAJOR and MINOR INTERVALS.

> If a perfect or a major interval is expanded by a half step it becomes <u>augmented</u>.

Examples:

P4	A4	P5	A5	M2	A2	M6	A6

If a perfect interval is contracted by a half step, it then becomes diminished; While if a major interval is contracted a half step, it becomes minor.

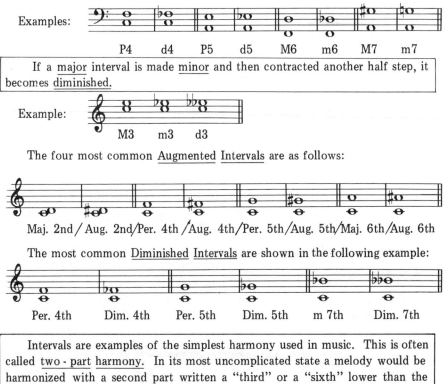

Examples:

P4 d4 P5 d5 M6 m6 M7 m7

If a major interval is made minor and then contracted another half step, it becomes diminished.

Example:

M3 m3 d3

The four most common Augmented Intervals are as follows:

Maj. 2nd / Aug. 2nd/Per. 4th /Aug. 4th/Per. 5th/Aug. 5th/Maj. 6th/Aug. 6th

The most common Diminished Intervals are shown in the following example:

Per. 4th   Dim. 4th   Per. 5th   Dim. 5th   m 7th   Dim. 7th

Intervals are examples of the simplest harmony used in music. This is often called two - part harmony. In its most uncomplicated state a melody would be harmonized with a second part written a "third" or a "sixth" lower than the melody.

Examples: (The second part is written a "third" lower.)

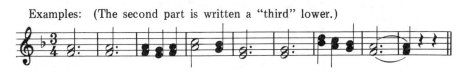

(The second part is written a "sixth" lower.)

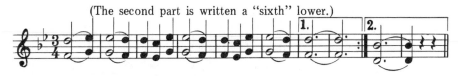

The inversion of an interval is the result of moving one of the tones an octave while the other tone remains stationary. When an interval is inverted, its character is changed.

When intervals are inverted:

1. These changes take place in the interval name.
   prime (or unison) becomes octave   fifth becomes fourth
   second becomes seventh   sixth becomes third
   third becomes sixth   seventh becomes second
   fourth becomes fifth   octave becomes prime (or unison)

2. The qualities change as follows:
   major becomes minor   diminished becomes augmented
   minor becomes major   augmented becomes diminished

3. All qualities are reversed except perfect.

Examples:

M3   m6   P5   P4   d5   A4   A4   d5

Remember: Adjustments in an interval may be made with either the top or bottom tone!!

(For more information and drills on Intervals and two-part harmony, see Theory and Harmony for Everyone, published by Mel Bay Publications, Inc.)

Intervals And Two-Part Harmony
(Review)

1. Write five examples of each of the following intervals. MINOR THIRD: MAJOR SECOND: MINOR SIXTH: MAJOR SEVENTH.

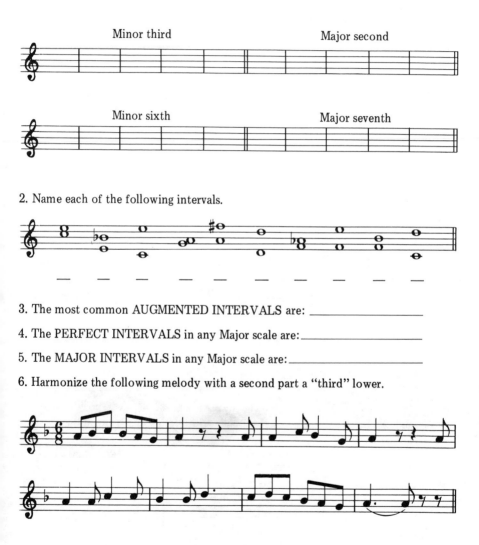

Minor third   Major second

Minor sixth   Major seventh

2. Name each of the following intervals.

3. The most common AUGMENTED INTERVALS are: _____

4. The PERFECT INTERVALS in any Major scale are: _____

5. The MAJOR INTERVALS in any Major scale are: _____

6. Harmonize the following melody with a second part a "third" lower.

Transposition

Transposition is the act of changing music from one key to another key. The most widely used method of transposition is by interval. Very often, the purpose of transposition is to enable a performer to use one system of fingering for a whole family of differently pitched instruments. (In band or orchestral music, for example.) The interval of transposition is measured on the Grand Staff. (See preceding chapter for a discussion of intervals.)

In the following example we will transpose a short phrase from the Key of E♭ Major to the Key of G Major. Because the key of G Major is a third higher than the Key of E♭ Major, we will write each note of the melody a third higher.

All orchestral or band music today is written on one of four clefs. The treble (G) and Bass (F) clefs, of course, and also on one of two C clefs; the Alto and Tenor. The Alto clef (often called the Viola clef), is made by combining the two lower lines of the G clef, "middle C", and the two upper lines of the F clef. This portion of the Grand Staff is thus isolated on a staff of its own.

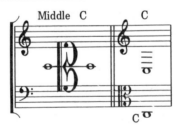

The Tenor Clef is constructed by taking the lowest line of the G clef, "Middle C", and the three upper lines of the F clef. This portion of the Grand Staff is isolated on a staff of its own.

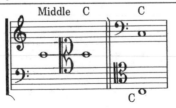

The Tenor Clef is often used by the cello, string bass, trombone, bassoon, and baritone horn.

A transposing instrument is one which sounds a pitch other than the one it reads. Another way to say it would be - it reads pitches other than it sounds. Instruments are very often labelled by the pitch of the scale they sound when they read a "C" scale. A B♭ instrument is one which sounds a B♭ scale when it reads a "C" scale. An E♭ is an instrument which sounds an E♭ scale when it reads a "C" scale. The interval of transposition in measured from "Middle C". Therefore, in order to be able to play "in tune" with the concert pitch, the composer or arranger must transpose some instruments the same interval above or below the concert pitch that the instrument sounds above or below that pitch.

The B♭ Soprano instruments include Clarinets, Cornets, Trumpets, and Saxophones. They sound a major second below "Middle C", so they must be written a major second above Middle C".

The A soprano instruments include clarinets, cornets, trumpets, and sometimes, French Horns. They sound a minor third below "Middle C", so they must be written a minor third above "Middle C".

Some additional transposing instruments are as follows:

Instruments	Group Includes:	They sound:	They must be written:
G Alto Instruments	Alto Flute; sometimes French Horn	Perfect fourth below concert pitch	a perfect fourth above concert pitch
F Alto Instruments	French Horn; English Horn; Mellophone; some Saxophones	perfect fifth below concert pitch	a perfect fifth above concert pitch
E♭ Alto Instruments	Alto Saxophones; French Horns; Alto Horns; Mellophones	major sixth below concert pitch	a major sixth above concert pitch
C Tenor Instruments	Bass Flute; Baritone Oboe	octave below written pitch	no transposition necessary

Transposition
(Review)

1. Transpose the following melody from the key of G to the keys indicated.

2. Rewrite the following melody onto the alto clef.

3. Transpose this melody for G alto instruments to sound in unison with concert pitch.

(For more information and <u>drills</u> On Transposition, See <u>Theory and Harmony for Everyone</u> published by Mel Bay Publications, Inc.)

Triads–Chords

A <u>chord</u> consists of two or more tones sounded together. A <u>triad</u> is a chord using three tones.

There are four types of triads: major, minor, augmented, and diminished.

A major chord or triad contains a root, a major third, and a perfect fifth.

The following are
major triads:

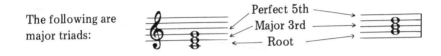

If we build a chord consisting of a root-third-fifth on every degree of a major scale, we will find three major chords.

In the following example, notice the use of ROMAN NUMERALS to help identify the scale degree.

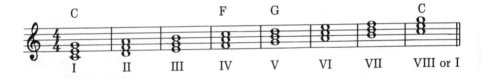

The three major chords occur on the first, I; fourth, IV; and fifth, V, degrees of the major scale.

Each scale degree has a name as well as a number. The first degree, which gives the tone of the key, is called the <u>Tonic.</u> The fifth degree is the "dominating" note of the scale, and is called the <u>Dominant.</u> The fourth degree is called the <u>Sub-dominant.</u> These three degrees are often referred to by name and are often called the <u>primary</u> or <u>principal</u> triads.

35

The names of all the scale degrees are as follows:

First Degree - Tonic
Second Degree - Supertonic
Third Degree - Mediant
Fourth Degree - Subdominant
Fifth Degree - Dominant
Sixth Degree - Submediant
Seventh Degree - Leading Tone
Eighth Degree - Octave

Chords may be written in different positions. The original position always has the root at the bottom. Other positions are called <u>Inversions.</u>

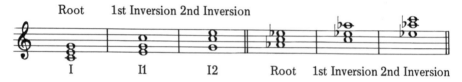

Simple choral harmony is usually written in four voices or parts. One way to do this would be to write the root of each chord in the bass. Since there are only three notes in a Tonic or a Dominant chord, one tone (usually the root) must be doubled. The movement of one chord to another is called a <u>progression</u>. In many progressions there is a common tone. It is usually best to keep the common tone in the same voice.

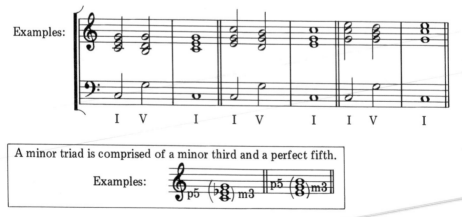

A minor triad is comprised of a minor third and a perfect fifth.

Minor Triads occur on the second, II; third, III; and sixth, VI, degrees of the major scale.

The following are various inversions of the minor triads in the key of C Major.

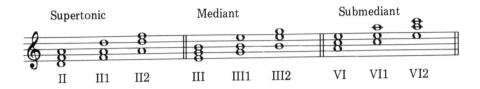

Supertonic			Mediant			Submediant		
II	II1	II2	III	III1	III2	VI	VI1	VI2

> Remember: a chord is inverted when any note other than the root is in the bass. When the fifth of any triad is in the bass, it is called a six-four chord. Inversions of the minor triads are figured the same as major triads.

An augmented triad is comprised of a major third and an augmented fifth.

Examples:

A diminished triad is comprised of a minor third and a diminished fifth.

Examples:

> On the following pages a limited amount of information is included about more complex chords. For exercises and drills in the use of these chords or for more detailed information on their use, see Theory and Harmony for Everyone published by Mel Bay Publications, Inc., Pacific, Mo. 63069.

If we add a minor seventh to the Dominant or V chord, it is then called the DOMINANT SEVENTH and is marked V7. The figure 7 may also be used after the letter name. (For example: C7; G7; D7 -)

These are
DOMINANT
SEVENTH
CHORDS

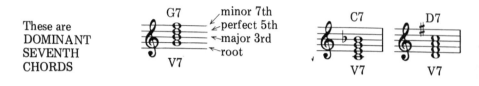

FACTS ABOUT THE DOMINANT SEVENTH:

The root of the Dominant Seventh chord may be written in the bass, and is usually doubled in the upper voices. The Dominant triad very often is before the Dominant Seventh. The Dominant Seventh may be repeated in a different position before resolving. Because of the minor seventh interval, the Dominant Seventh chord is more strongly attracted than the Dominant triad, towards the Tonic. It is used more often before the Tonic at the end of a phrase.

The <u>Minor Seventh chord</u> is formed by adding the minor seventh interval to the minor triad. It is composed of a root, a minor third, a perfect fifth, and a minor seventh. The symbol is Am7 or Ami7.

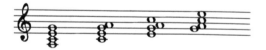

This chord contains both a major triad and its relative minor triad. In the <u>1st</u> inversion with the 3rd in the bass, it becomes major in quality. In the <u>2nd</u> and <u>3rd</u> inversions it is minor in quality as it is, of course, in its original position with the root in the bass.

The <u>Dominant Ninth chord</u> is formed by adding the major ninth interval to the dominant seventh chord. It has the same inversions as the dominant seventh, and may be used instead. In four part harmony, the root, third or fifth is omitted. The ninth is usually found in the top voice, rarely the root.

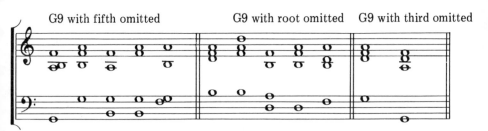

G9 with fifth omitted   G9 with root omitted   G9 with third omitted

The <u>Diminished Seventh chord</u> is composed of a root, a minor third, a diminished fifth and a diminished seventh. Example 1 is the correct notation of a Diminished Seventh on C.

Exp. 1   C dim.

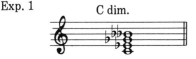

Because the correct notation is usually hard to read, "enharmonic equivalents" are used.

Exp. 2

The <u>Augmented Fifth chord</u> is composed of a root, a major third and an augmented fifth. It resolves to the major or minor triad of which the root is the dominant. Enharmonically there are only four of these chords. Therefore any note of the chord could be the root. In four part harmony, the root is usually doubled, sometimes the third, but seldom the fifth. Study the following examples!

Caug.   F   B♭ aug. E♭   F aug. B♭   G aug. C   G aug. C

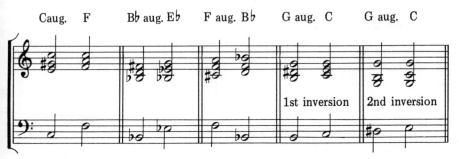

1st inversion   2nd inversion

39

Triads–Chords
(Review)

1. Build a major chord on the first, fourth, and fifth degrees of the following keys. Mark the Roman Numeral below and the letter name above each chord.

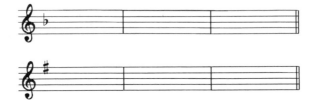

2. Fill in the missing note in the following major chords. Since there is no key signature indicated, it will be necessary to write in the proper accidentals (sharps or flats).

3. Write a Major, minor, augmented, and diminished triad on each of the following notes.

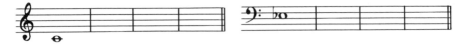

4. Harmonize the following melody.

Chord Progressions

Traditionally there have been several basic rules governing the progression of chords and chord sequences. To cover this area thoroughly one should use books that are totally devoted to harmony. In this particular book we will mention only the most common of the rules. Composition and harmonization of melodies takes much time and practice. The serious student should continue to work on his own remembering that, except for certain fundamental principles, there are no hard and fast rules.

1. A chord may progress to another chord whose root is either a perfect fourth above or a perfect fifth below. In modern harmony, the VII chord is treated as a V7 chord, with the root missing.
The progression of chord roots through the cycle of fifths is called Normal or Harmonic. This is often found in a series or sequential pattern.

Exp.

2. A chord may progress to another chord whose root is either a perfect fifth above or a perfect fourth below.
3. All major, minor or seventh chords built on degrees of a major scale are relative to its key.
4. A chord may progress to another chord whose root is either a major or minor third above or a major or minor third below.
5. An accidental in the melody sometimes indicates the third of a new chord. It is usually better to have contrary motion between the bass and melody. This sometimes calls for an inverted chord.
6. A chord may progress to another chord whose root is either a major or minor second above or a major or minor second below. When the root interval is a minor second, the chord progression is usually chromatic.
7. In harmonizing a melody, it should be kept in mind that one should finish with some form of the tonic chord.

Final Review

1. Under the following notes write the letter name of the note.

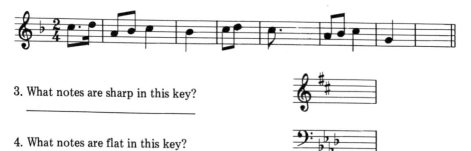

— — — — — — —   — — — — — — —

2. Complete the time values in the following measures, using either notes or rests.

3. What notes are sharp in this key?
_____

4. What notes are flat in this key?
_____

5. Name the notes in the following exercise, (Note the key signature!)

E — —   — — —   — — —

6. The interval between any two tones of a chromatic scale is a _____.
7. Two or more notes differing in name but sounding the same pitch are called
_____ tones.
8. Match the following signs with their correct definition:
   A - D.C.   _____ from the sign
   B - rit.   _____ gradually louder
   C - dim.   _____ coda sign
   D - ⊕   _____ gradually softer
   E - D.S.   _____ from the beginning
   F - cresc.   _____ gradually slower
9. Name the three relative minor scales: _____ , _____ , _____ ,
10. All minor scales begin on the _____ degree of their relative major scales:

11. Transpose the following melody from F Major to A Major.

12. Identify the following perfect and major intervals:

13. Harmonize the following bass passage.

14. Harmonize the following melody.

Chord Building Chart[*]

Chord Type	Scale Degrees Used	Symbols
Major	Root, 3rd, 5th	Maj
Minor	Root, ♭3rd, 5th	mi, –,m
Diminished	Root, ♭3rd, ♭5th, ♭♭7th	dim, °
Augmented	Root, 3rd, ♯5th	+, aug.
Dominant Seventh	Root, 3rd, 5th, ♭7th	dom. 7, 7
Minor Seventh	Root, ♭3rd, 5th, ♭7th	–7, min 7
Major Seventh	Root, 3rd, 5th, maj. 7th	M7, ma 7
Major Sixth	Root, 3rd, 5th, 6th	M6, M6, 6
Minor Sixth	Root, ♭3rd, 5th, 6th	mi 6,–6
Seventh ♯5th	Root, 3rd, ♯5th, ♭7th	7^{+5}, $7^{♯5}$
Seventh ♭5th	Root, 3rd, ♭5th, ♭7th	7^{-5}, $7^{♭5}$
Major 7th ♭3rd	Root, ♭3rd, 5th, maj. 7th	$Ma\ 7^{-3}$
Minor 7th ♭5th	Root, ♭3rd, ♭5th, ♭7th	$mi\ 7^{-5}$,$7^{♭5}$
Seventh Suspended 4th	Root, 4th, 5th, ♭7th	7 sus 4
Ninth	Root, 3rd, 5th, ♭7th, 9th	9
Minor Ninth	Root, ♭3rd, 5th, ♭7th, 9th	mi 9,–9
Major Ninth	Root, 3rd, 5th, maj. 7th, 9th	Ma 9
Ninth Augmented 5th	Root, 3rd, ♯5th, ♭7th, 9th	$9^{♯5}$, $9^{♯5}$
Ninth Flatted 5th	Root, 3rd, ♭5th, ♭7th, 9th	9^{-5}, $9^{♭5}$
Seventh ♭9	Root, 3rd, 5th, ♭7th, ♭9th	7^{-9}, $7^{♭9}$
Augmented Ninth	Root, 3rd, 5th, ♭7th, ♯9th	9^{+}_{+}, 7^{+9}
9/6	Root, 3rd, 5th, 6th, 9th	$^9_6$, 6 add 9
Eleventh	Root, 3rd, 5th, ♭7th, 9th, 11th	11
Augmented Eleventh	Root, 3rd, 5th, ♭7th, 9th, ♯11th	11^{+}, 7 aug 11
Thirteenth	Root, 3rd, 5th, ♭7th, 9th, 11th, 13th	13
Thirteenth ♭9	Root, 3rd, 5th, ♭7th, ♭9th, 11th, 13th	$13^{♭9}$
Thirteenth ♭9♭5	Root, 3rd, ♭5th, ♭7th, ♭9th, 11th, 13th	$13^{♭9♭5}$
Half Diminished	Root, ♭3rd, ♭5th, ♭7th	Ø

*Note - To arrive at scale degrees above 1 octave (i.e., 9th, 11th, 13th) continue your scale up 2 octaves and keep numbering. The 2nd scale degree will be 9th tone as you begin your second octave.

Chromatic Fingering Chart For Guitar

(Lines Connect Identical Notes Found On Different Strings)

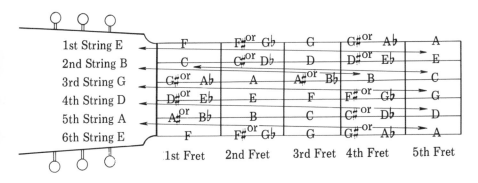

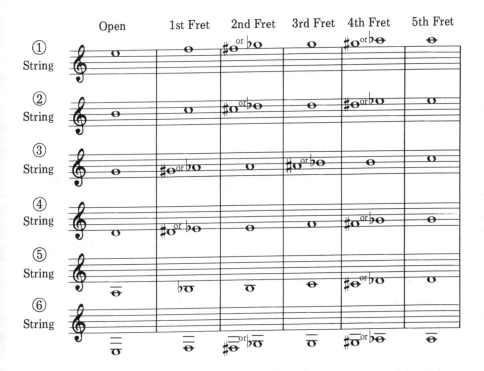

Definitions Of Musical Terms

Accelerando	Gradually increasing the rate of speed.
Accent	Emphasis upon a certain note or beat.
Accidentals	All signs for raising or lowering the pitch that are not found in the key signature.
Adagio	To play slowly.
Allegro	To play at a high rate of speed, though not so fast as presto.
Allegro con moto	Fast, with movement.
Allegro moderato	Moderately fast.
Andante	Play in moderate time.
Animato	Animated or lively.
Bar (bar line)	A line drawn through the staff to show the division of the time in a piece of music. The space between two bar lines is called a measure.
Bar, double	Heavy double lines drawn through the staff, usually to designate the end of a section or of a composition.
Beat	The regular underlying pulsation in a piece of music.
Cadence	The chordal progression at the end of a phrase, section or composition.
Chord	An organized vertical combination of musical sounds.
Chromatic	A chord, interval or scale which includes notes not belonging to the regular diatonic scale.
Clef	The sign placed at the beginning of a piece of music to fix the pitch or the position of one note, and consequently of the rest. The most common clefs are treble clef and bass clef.
Crescendo	Gradually getting louder or to increase the force of sound.
Decrescendo	To get softer or to decrease the volume of sound.
Diatonic	The tones or the notes of the standard major or minor scale.
Diminuendo	To become softer
Dissonance	A discord
Dominant	The name applied to the fifth note of the scale.

Duple (double)	Two beats to the measure.
Embellishment	The ornaments of melody (i.e., trill or turn)
Enharmonic	Having intervals less than a semitone
Fermata	Hold
Fine	The end.
Flat	Lowers the pitch of the note a semitone.
Frets	Small strips of wood, ivory or metal placed upon the fingerboard of certain stringed instruments (i.e., guitar or banjo).
Harmony	The art of combining pitches or tones into chords.
Improvisation	"On the spur of the moment," an extemporaneous performance.
Interval	The difference in pitch between two tones.
Key	The series of tones forming any major or minor scale.
Largo	Very slowly.
Ledger lines	The short additional lines drawn above or below the staff.
Legato	Smoothly and connected.
Maestoso	Majestically
Major scale	The scale which has semitones between the third and fourth and seventh and eighth degrees.
Marcato	To play with emphasis.
Measure	The portion of the music enclosed between two bar lines.
Melody	A succession of tones arranged rhythmically and symmetrically.
Minor scale	The scale formed by lowering the third and sixth degree of the major scale one-half step.
Modulation	The movement from one key to another by an organized succession of chords.
Natural	The character used to cancel a sharp or a flat.
Notation	In general, any musical sign (i.e., the staff, clef, notes, or rests)
Octave	Eight notes above or below the interval of an eighth.

Pitch	The heighth or depth of a tone expressed in number or vibrations per second.
Poco a poco	Little by little
Presto	Rapidly
Rallentando	Gradually getting slower
Repeat	A sign which indicates that certain measures or sections are to be performed twice.
Rests	Signs which indicate silence.
Rhythm	The organized arrangement of sound and silence.
Scale	A series of consecutive tones proceeding by half steps (chromatic) or by half steps and whole steps (major or minor)
Sharp	The sign which raises the pitch of a note one half step.
Signature	The sign such as sharps and flats placed at the beginning of a piece of music to show the key.
Slur	A curved line placed over notes directing that they be played legato.
Sostenuto	To sustain the tone
Staccato	To play in a crisp and detached manner.
Stem	The line attached to a note - head
Subito	Suddenly
Syncopation	To accent a normally unaccented beat, or to shift the accent from a strong beat to a weak beat.
Tablature	A system of notation used for certain stringed instruments (i.e., guitar or banjo)
Tempo	Rate of movement or speed of music
Tie	A curved line joining two notes of the same pitch and adding the duration of the second note to the first.
Transpose	To perform or to write a compositon in a different key.
Triad	The common chord of three notes
Unison	Pitches having the same number of vibrations per second.
Vivace	Lively.